RAND

A Tutorial and Exercises for the Compensation, Accessions, and Personnel Management (CAPM) Model

John Ausink, Albert A. Robbert

Prepared for the
United States Air Force and
the Office of the Secretary of Defense

Project AIR FORCE and National Defense Research Institute

The research reported here was sponsored by the United States Air Force and by the Office of the Secretary of Defense (OSD). The research was conducted in RAND's Project AIR FORCE, a federally funded research and development center sponsored by the United States Air Force under Contract F49642-01-C-0003, and in RAND's National Defense Research Institute, a federally funded research and development center supported by the OSD, the Joint Staff, the unified commands, and the defense agencies under Contract DASW01-01-C-0004.

Library of Congress Cataloging-in-Publication Data

Ausink, John A.
    A tutorial and exercises for the compensation, accessions, and personnel management (CAPM) model / John A. Ausink, Albert A. Robbert.
        p. cm.
    Includes bibliographical references.
    "MR-1669."
    ISBN 0-8330-3430-8 (pbk.)
    1. United States—Armed Forces—Recruiting, enlistment, etc.—Mathematical models—Problems, exercises, etc. 2. United States—Armed Forces—Pay, allowances, etc.—Evaluation—Problems, exercises, etc. 3. United States—Armed Forces—Personnel management—Mathematical models—Problems, exercises, etc. 4. Employee retention—United states—Mathematical models—Problems, exercises, etc. I. Robbert, Albert A., 1944– II.Title.

UB323.A9424 2003
355.6'1'0973—dc21

2003014002

RAND is a nonprofit institution that helps improve policy and decisionmaking through research and analysis. RAND® is a registered trademark. RAND's publications do not necessarily reflect the opinions or policies of its research sponsors.

Published 2003 by RAND
1700 Main Street, P.O. Box 2138, Santa Monica, CA 90407-2138
1200 South Hayes Street, Arlington, VA 22202-5050
201 North Craig Street, Suite 202, Pittsburgh, PA 15213-1516
RAND URL: http://www.rand.org/
To order RAND documents or to obtain additional information, contact Distribution Services: Telephone: (310) 451-7002; Fax: (310) 451-6915; Email: order@rand.org

Preface

The Compensation, Accessions, and Personnel Management (CAPM) system[1] provides action officers and analysts with a powerful tool for exploring the interaction of policy and behavioral variables in enlisted force management. This document demonstrates the model's capabilities in tutorial format and shows how CAPM can be used to model some prototypical policy issues. Its primary purpose is to help users explore capabilities of the model and gain confidence in manipulating its parameters. It is one of three RAND reports that describe the CAPM 2.2 software. The other two documents are *Background and Theory Behind the Compensation, Accessions, and Personnel Management (CAPM) Model* (MR-1667-AF/OSD) and *Users' Guide for the Compensation, Accessions, and Personnel Management (CAPM) Model* (MR-1668-AF/OSD).

The initial research for CAPM was sponsored by the Assistant Secretary of Defense (Force Management and Personnel) from 1991 to 1994; follow-on work from 1999 to 2001 was jointly sponsored by that office and by the Deputy Chief of Staff, Personnel, Headquarters, U.S. Air Force. This research was conducted within the Forces and Resources Policy Center of RAND's National Defense Research Institute (NDRI) and the Manpower, Personnel, and Training Program of RAND's Project AIR FORCE (PAF). This document is directed toward managers and analysts who are interested in using CAPM 2.2 software to analyze the effects of changes in personnel compensation policy.

National Defense Research Institute

RAND's NDRI is a federally funded research and development center sponsored by the Office of the Secretary of Defense, the Joint Staff, the unified commands, and the defense agencies.

Project AIR FORCE

PAF, another division of RAND, is the U.S. Air Force's federally funded research and development center for studies and analyses. It provides the Air Force with

---

[1]Throughout this report, "CAPM," "CAPM model," and "CAPM system" will be used interchangeably to refer to the software package as a whole.

independent analyses of policy alternatives affecting the development, employment, combat readiness, and support of current and future aerospace forces. Research is performed in four programs: Aerospace Force Development; Manpower, Personnel, and Training; Resource Management; and Strategy and Doctrine.

Additional information about PAF is available on our web site at http://www.rand.org/paf.

Contents

vi

Appendix

Figures

Tables

Summary

The motivation for the development of the Compensation, Accessions, and Personnel Management (CAPM) model was to provide a theoretically sound, relatively easy-to-use analytical tool that would enable decisionmakers to study the effects of changes in personnel policy. Jonathan Cave originally called CAPM an "architecture" because it is not simply a computer model; it is an Excel®-based analytic structure that includes databases, modules written in Visual Basic for Applications, a graphic user interface, and a variety of tools to analyze model output.[1]

This tutorial guides the reader through five exercises using CAPM in order to show how the model can be manipulated and how results can be interpreted. After describing the process of setting up a "base" case for analysis, the tutorial uses the exercises to explore the effects of the following personnel policies:

- Changing the demographic composition of accessions.
- Introducing voluntary loss incentives.
- Modifying pay tables.
- Using "targeted" bonuses.
- Limiting cost of living adjustments for retired pay.

These exercises are applied to the Air Force population as a whole. The tutorial concludes with a description of how similar analyses could be conducted for populations defined at the three-digit Air Force Specialty Code level.

Finally, an appendix provides January 2000 Air Force pay tables by years of service and grade.

---

[1]Throughout this report, "CAPM," "CAPM model," and "CAPM system" will be used interchangeably to refer to the software package as a whole.

Acknowledgments

Al Robbert wrote the original version of this tutorial for a 1994 release of CAPM. Saul Pleeter, Colonel Dave Moore, and William Carr, who were all in the Office of the Assistant Secretary of Defense for Force Management Policy at the time, suggested the scenarios used in that version. This document illustrates the updated capabilities of CAPM 2.2, but the basic approach to the tutorial comes from Al's earlier work. RAND colleague Tom Manacapilli was instrumental in updating CAPM software and improving its capabilities. Jerry Ball, formerly of RAND and now at the Air Force Personnel Center, made excellent suggestions that improved the presentation of the material. The careful reading of Craig Moore, director of Project AIR FORCE's Manpower, Personnel, and Training program, helped make the tutorial better. We are grateful to Glenn Gotz and Michael Mattock, who served as reviewers for this work. Their insights and suggestions greatly improved the final version of this document.

Acronyms and Abbreviations

ACOL	Annualized cost of leaving
AFSC	Air Force Specialty Code
CAPM	Compensation, Accessions, and Personnel Management
COLA	Cost of living adjustment
ETS	End of term of service
FY	Fiscal year
High-3	Highest three earnings years
NPS	Non-prior service
RMC	Regular military compensation
SSB	Selective separation bonus
TERA	Temporary Early Retirement Authority
WMH	White, male, high mental category
WML	White, male, low mental category
YOS	Years of service

1. Introduction

Background

This document demonstrates how to use the Compensation, Accessions, and Personnel Management (CAPM)[1] modeling system to gain insight into a variety of issues commonly encountered in defense manpower management. Like any model, CAPM is a simplified representation of a more complex reality. Those who are familiar with the "territory"—analysts, programmers, and action officers who have been involved in some aspect of wholesale or corporate-level military personnel management—will most readily recognize the features represented in the model. The tutorial is oriented primarily to this audience. Others may be learning some of this territory at the same time they are learning the model. The tutorial attempts in a more limited way to meet some of the needs of this audience as well.

CAPM is implemented in a Microsoft Excel spreadsheet environment, and the tutorial assumes that the user has at least a rudimentary knowledge of Excel file and cell manipulation, including familiarity with pivot tables. This tutorial is based on a developmental version of CAPM 2.2 and Microsoft Excel 97, and the exercises use calendar year 2000 as the most recently available base year—the year that provides the starting inventory, historical reenlistment rates, promotion rates, and other beginning arguments for the model's projections.[2]

Objectives and Approach

CAPM was designed to integrate three areas of policy (compensation, accessions, and personnel management) into one system to enable an analyst to easily study the potential effects of proposed policy changes. The exercises in this tutorial focus on personnel and compensation issues, with accession consequences discussed in the context of how the model operates. While this is a tutorial on

---

[1] Throughout this report, "CAPM," "CAPM model," and "CAPM system" will be used interchangeably to refer to the software package as a whole.

[2] Air Force data from calendar year 2000 were used for inventories, continuation rates, reenlistment rates, and promotion rates. Pay tables from January 2001 were used to calculate default annualized cost of leaving (ACOL) values. Default ACOL values used a value of 0.053 for the overall inflation rate and for the civilian pay inflation rate.

using CAPM, it is not a basic introduction to the CAPM computer model itself. Novice CAPM users can learn more about model details by consulting the CAPM users' guide (MR-1668-AF/OSD).

Outline of the Document

The remainder of this document is divided into three sections. Within each section, illustrative policy issues are explored using the model and any necessary outside references. Each policy treatment will include a general description of the problem, step-by-step instructions for modifying parameters and operating the model, and an examination and interpretation of selected results. For two reasons, users are encouraged to review the examples in each of the policy areas, even if their interest lies primarily in only one of them. First, since policy variables of interest in one sphere may affect other areas, users should try to develop some understanding of those incidental effects. Second, step-by-step instructions will be more detailed in the earlier examples in the document. Thus, those interested in policy areas treated in later sections might find the earlier sections useful for learning to navigate within the model.

Section 2 contains exercises in personnel management. These are presented first because they encompass the most straightforward application of CAPM's inventory projection model. Exercises in compensation management introduce several additional complexities and are presented in Section 3. These exercises require manipulation of ancillary files or parameter inputs used by one of CAPM's underlying behavioral models. A very brief fourth section discusses disaggregate analysis of individual Air Force Specialty Codes (AFSCs) and CAPM's steady-state feature.

In addition to providing a way of systematically exploring the capabilities of the CAPM model, the exercises presented here will suggest ways of simulating common policy issues within CAPM's framework.

Note for the First-Time User

The most recent version of CAPM is available on the web at www.rand.org/ publications/MR/MR1668/. Appendix A of the CAPM users' guide (MR-1668-AF/OSD) contains instructions for installing CAPM 2.2 and describes the program's directories and files. To use this tutorial, your computer should have a folder named "CAPM" that contains

1. subfolders named "User" and "Data"

2. two program files named Capm.xls and firsttime.xls

3. a data file named Rand2000.xls

4. three template files named Scenario.xlt, Accession.xlt, and Comp.xlt.

The "Data" subfolder should contain three files named Policy.db, USAF.dbg, and Payalt.db. CAPM will send its output files to the "User" subfolder.

If this is the first time CAPM 2.2 has been used on your computer, you should run the "firsttime.xls" file (located in the CAPM root directory) before doing anything else. This program ensures that some Excel routines are loaded and that data paths are set up properly. After doing this, you should save CAPM in order to ensure that you do not have to run firsttime.xls the next time you use the model.

2. Personnel Management

One of CAPM's strengths is its flexibility to model a wide variety of force-shaping policies. To illustrate this capability, we will consider two examples that shape the force in different ways. One adjusts the composition of accessions; the other creates incentives for certain people to leave the service. In both examples, we will start with a year 2000 inventory and age the force from 2001 to 2004.

In these examples, and those to follow, the analysis consists of five basic steps. While the process of modifying the parameters or changing the output views may become complex for some policies, it will be helpful to keep these steps in mind:

- Define a baseline case in terms of the model's parameters.
- Run the model using those parameters and save the results.
- Modify the model's parameters to reflect a policy of interest.
- Run the model using the modified parameters and save the results.
- Compare the results of the two runs using CAPM's built-in comparison routines and interpret their meaning.

Changing the Composition of Accessions

Defining a Baseline Case

The first step in this exercise is to establish a baseline scenario, a base case that generally accepts the default parameters provided by CAPM and models the force as though there were no strong force structuring policies in effect. The only parameter changes we will make prior to running the model will be to set the base, initial, and final dates used by the model.

The base date sets the year from which the starting inventory, loss rates, and other model inputs are derived. The initial and final dates set the years through which the force is aged. For this exercise, as indicated above, we will use 2000 as the base year, 2001 as the initial year, and 2004 as the final year. We begin the exercise by opening a new scenario sheet.[1]

- From the CAPM screen (shown in Figure 2.1), click New (for a new scenario) on the CAPM toolbar at the bottom of the screen. This will open a scenario sheet such as the one shown in Figure 2.2. The upper left of your screen will show the name "ScenarioX," where X is the number of the sheet opened during your CAPM session.
- On the scenario sheet, click Initialize Data.
- In the resulting dialogue box (Figure 2.3), select the service (Air Force) by clicking on the up or down arrows until "USAF" appears. In the "Dates" section, enter 2001 as the initial date, 2004 as the final date, and 2000 as the base date. In the "Reenlistment method" section, select "ACOL II coefficients" and "Delta method." For "Label," select a label such as "afhist1" (indicating that this is an Air Force scenario, run from a historical database, first iteration). (NOTE: While you will choose your own labels during "real world" use of the model, it will simplify your use of this tutorial if you follow the suggested names while you are working through it.)

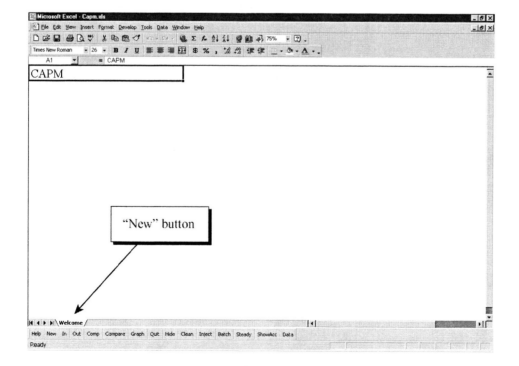

Figure 2.1—CAPM Screen

---

[1]When you need to discontinue work with CAPM, you should use Quit on the CAPM toolbar rather than exiting Excel in the usual manner, to ensure that the model shuts down properly.

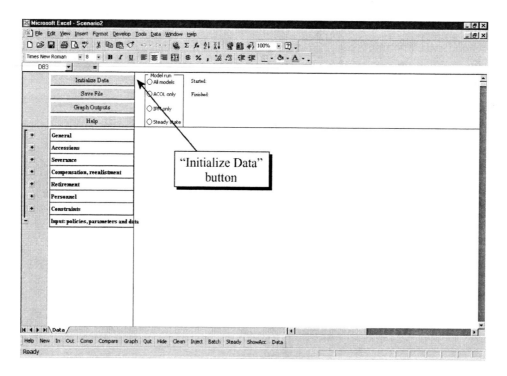

Figure 2.2—CAPM Scenario Sheet

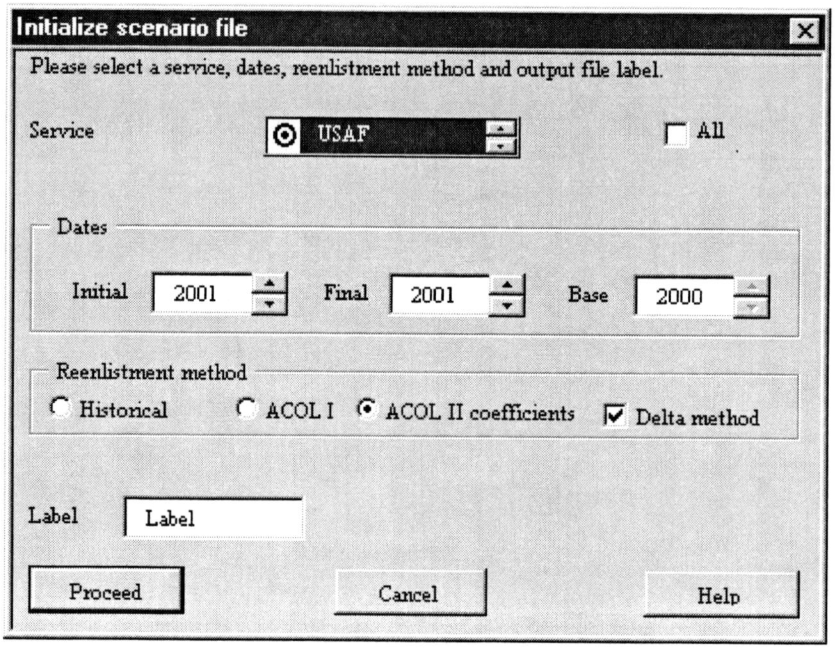

Figure 2.3—Scenario Initialization Dialogue Box

- Click ⎡Proceed⎤. At the bottom left of the screen you will see some rapidly changing messages indicating that CAPM is setting up various data ranges in preparation for calculations. When the setup is complete, you will see a scenario sheet such as the one in Figure 2.4.

- After CAPM sets up the files and ranges it needs, the default policy parameters used by the model will be contained in the scenario sheet indexed by the headings in the left column. If you click on ⎡+⎤ to the left of the "Input: policies, parameters and data" cell, it will open to show a variety of policy categories. Clicking on ⎡+⎤ next to the "General" category allows you to check that the label, service, and projection dates you desire were entered properly. This is shown in Figure 2.5.[2]

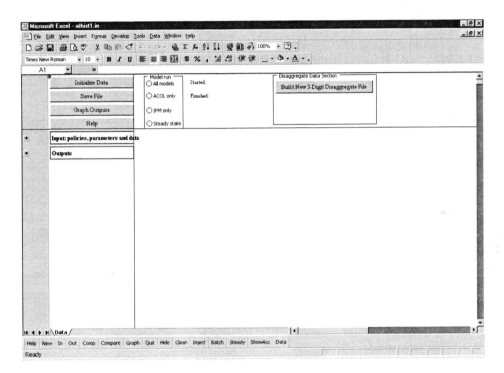

Figure 2.4—Scenario Sheet After Initialization

- The "Constraints" category contains all parameters, such as end strengths, that vary by fiscal year (FY). To examine these parameters:
  — Click on ⎡+⎤ to the left of the "Constraints" cell. You will see the matrix shown in Figure 2.6 with columns labeled from 2001 to 2004 and rows with information such as "Endstrength" and "Min NPS Accessions

_____

[2]If you see that something was not entered properly, you can click on the appropriate cell and correct it.

WMH" (for minimum non-prior-service [NPS] accessions, white male, "high" aptitude).

— Use the arrow keys to scroll through the matrix in order to get a feel for the type of information that can be modified.

— After reviewing the parameters, close the matrix by clicking on ⊟ to the left of the "Constraints" cell (or on any part of the line extending upward from ⊟).

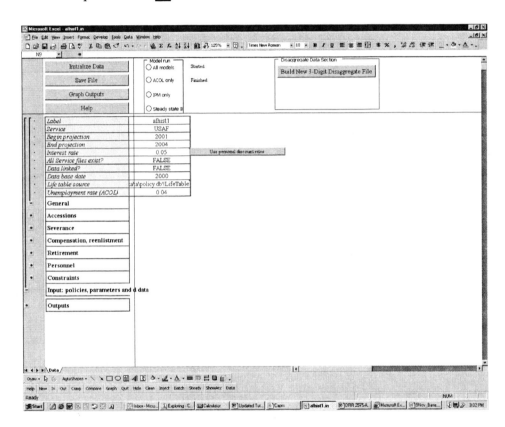

Figure 2.5—Opening the "General" Section of the "Inputs" Heading

We will modify policies in several categories in later exercises.

- For the baseline scenario, all default parameters will be accepted. No changes are needed in the "Input: policies, parameters and data" area of the scenario sheet.

Running the Baseline Model and Saving the Results

In the "Model run" box at the top of the scenario sheet, click the "All models" button. CAPM will start calculating inventories for the years 2001–2004. In the lower left of the screen you will see a series of rapidly changing messages that indicate the stage of processing. "Ready" will be displayed in the bottom left of the screen when the run has finished.

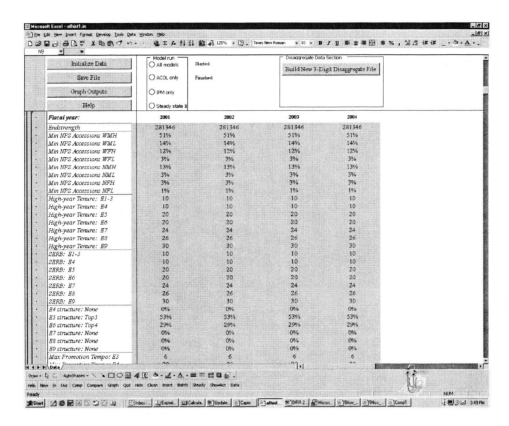

Figure 2.6—Scenario Sheet After Opening the "Constraints" Heading

After the run is completed, begin your examination of the outputs by checking the accession levels. To do this:

- Click on ⊞ next to "Outputs." Then click on ⊞ next to "NPS Accessions."

- A matrix of numbers for accessions will appear as in Figure 2.7, with one column for each year from 2001 to 2004.

- Note that there is a drop in accessions in 2002. This is because CAPM attempts to modify accessions so that the total inventory matches authorized end strength. Retention rates in 2001 are apparently high enough that the model can reduce accessions in 2002 and still maintain end strength.

- Click ⊞ next to the "Costs" cell to examine some of the costs associated with the forces projected by CAPM. This section shows the total regular military compensation (RMC) paid to the those in the inventory projected by the model, the retirement liability (the present value of retirement owed to those the model says have retired), and the retirement accrual (the bookkeeping

amount the government must take into account for *future* retirement
obligations to those in the current force).

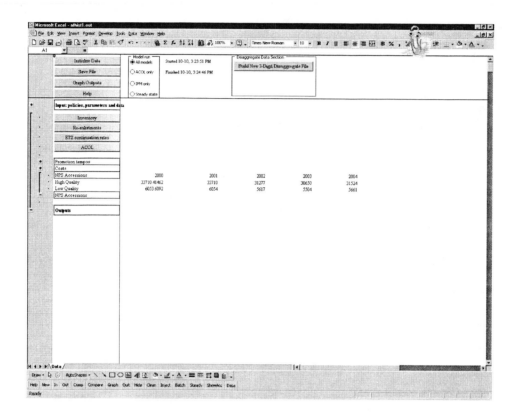

Figure 2.7—NPS Accessions Output

Modifying the Model's Parameters

In 1999, all services (except the Marine Corps) started expressing concern about
meeting recruiting goals. One response to this problem is to consider recruiting
more individuals with lower educational qualifications. We can explore possible
effects of such a policy by using CAPM to lower the accessions floor for
individuals in mental categories IIIA and above (labeled "High Quality" in the
model) and increase the percentage of individuals in mental categories IIIB and
below (labeled "Low Quality" in the model).[3,4]

---

[3]As discussed in the users' guide (MR-1668-AF/OSD), CAPM does not predict accessions; it
simply replaces losses with enough new personnel to maintain the desired end strength.

[4]"Mental category" is a technical term used for performance on the Armed Forces Qualification
Test. There are eight levels of performance. For example, "The policy of accessing quality active
duty enlisted personnel will be assessed by measuring the number of enlistees scoring in mental
categories I, II, and IIIa on the Armed Forces Qualification Test (AFQT)" according to AF Policy
Document 36-20, March 13, 2001. In CAPM, people in category IIIA and above are treated as "high"

To develop this scenario, click New at the bottom of the CAPM screen and then click "Initialize Data." Name the new scenario "afhist2" or something similar, select "USAF" as the service, and set the initial, final, and base years as 2001, 2004, and 2000, respectively. Hit Proceed to begin processing and to produce the afhist2.in screen.[5]

- Click next to the "Input: policies, parameters and data" cell to open the policy categories. Then click + next to the "General" cell and confirm that the input data you intended for label, for service, and for begin, end, and base dates are correct. Collapse the "General" cell by clicking on - and expand the "Constraints" cell by hitting + next to the label. Scroll to the top of the "Constraints" section. After the "Endstrength" line, the next eight rows contain default percentages of accessions for various demographic groups. The current percentages for white male, high-quality recruits and white male, low-quality recruits are 51 percent and 14 percent, respectively. Change the "Min NPS Accessions WMH" percentage to 40 percent and the "Min NPS Accessions WML" to 25 percent in each respective column. (NOTE: Enter 40 for 40 percent and 25 for 25 percent.) Having assured ourselves of the model's inputs, we are now ready to go to the next step.

Running the Model Using the Modified Parameters

- Click the "All models" button in the "Model run" box.

Comparing the Results of the Two Runs

Now that the baseline and alternative scenarios have been generated, CAPM's comparison feature may be used to examine the differences between them.

- Click Compare on the CAPM toolbar at the bottom of the screen, shown in Figure 2.8.

---

mental (or aptitude or quality) category. Those in categories IIIB and below are in the "low" mental category.

[5]CAPM will offer you the option to save any changes made to the output from the previous scenario. Excel will think you made changes even if you simply opened or closed a heading, so you can safely answer "no" to the option unless you really did make changes you want to save.

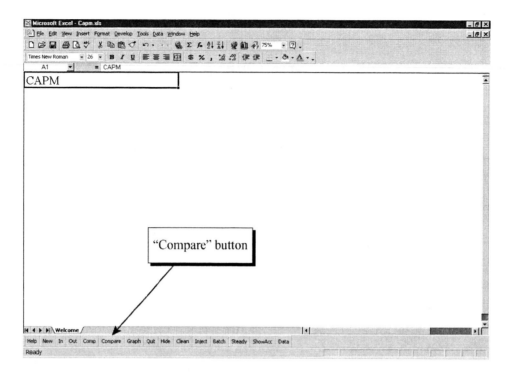

Figure 2.8—Compare Button

- In the large dialogue box that appears (see Figure 2.9), select "Automatically Save Results?" and insert a label, such as "afhist12," in the "Label for workbook(s)" box. In the "Basis for comparison" area, select "New – old" (meaning "new value minus old value"), which will provide simple differences between the two files.[6] The "Inventory for ACOL, Reenlistment Pivot Tables" section selects average as the default; leave that for now. Finally, select "Single pair of cases." If that option is already selected, click Proceed at the bottom of the dialogue box.

_____

[6]If you select "New – Old as % of:," CAPM calculates differences between the two files as a percentage of either the new value, the old value, or the average of new and old values. This can be useful for computing elasticities. See the users' guide (MR-1668-AF/OSD) for details.

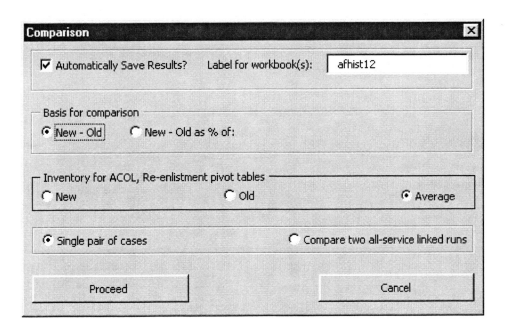

Figure 2.9—Comparison Dialogue Box

- In the next two dialogue boxes (which will be similar to the one shown in Figure 2.10), select *afhist2.out* as the "new" case and *afhist1.out* as the "old" case (or whatever labels you used for the alternative and baseline scenarios). CAPM will produce a workbook (called afhist12.xlw), such as the one shown in Figure 2.11, that displays several items of information. At the top of the sheet is a summary of the basis for the comparison: the name of the new file, the name of the old file, the first FY of the comparison, the last FY of the comparison,[7] the basis for the comparison, and the base inventory for the comparison.

---

[7] It is possible to compare two files that have a different number of years in the projection. The comparison file will have as its first year the *latest* initial date and as its last year the *earliest* final date. For example, if one projection runs from 1999 to 2004 and the other runs from 2000 to 2005, the comparison file will be from 2000 to 2004.

14

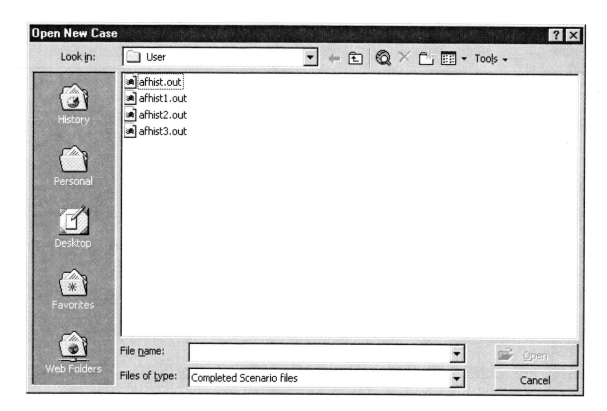

Figure 2.10—Selecting the New Case for Comparison

- Comparison data are contained in four pivot tables: inventory, reenlistments, ETS continuation rates,[8] and ACOL values. Pressing the appropriate button opens the corresponding pivot table. In addition to the pivot tables, promotion tempos, costs, and NPS accessions can be examined by clicking on ⊞ next to the appropriate cell in the worksheet.[9]

---

[8]ETS is end of term of service.

[9]If there is no ⊞ next to promotion tempos, costs, and NPS accessions, click on ⊟ to collapse everything to comparisons and then click on ⊞ to reexpand comparisons.

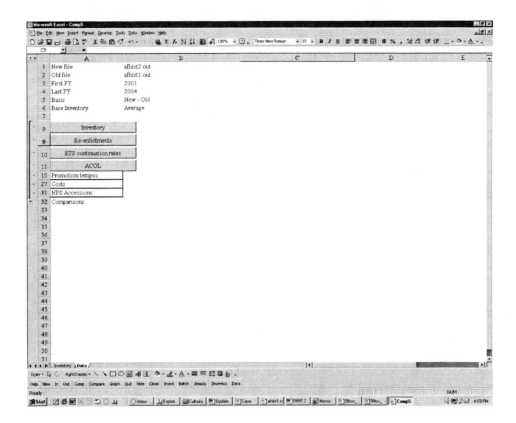

Figure 2.11—Data Worksheet of a Comparison Workbook

The Effect of Aptitude Changes on Inventory

Press Inventory on the comparison data worksheet. This will produce the pivot table shown in Figure 2.12, which displays inventories by grade and years of service (YOS). The comparison workbook initially calculates cell entries as weighted averages, with population being the weight. The "#DIV/0!" entries in the table are cells in which the population is zero.

16

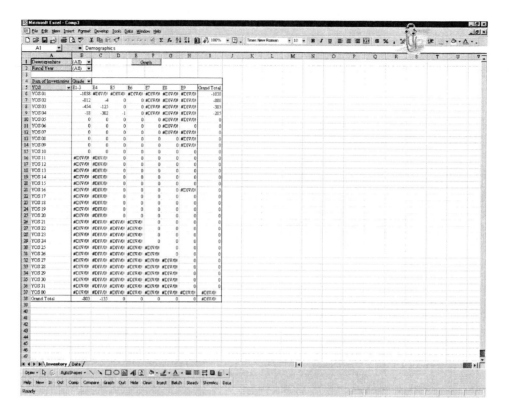

Figure 2.12—Inventory Pivot Table

Change the display to show inventory by years of service and fiscal year in the following way: Click on Fiscal year and drag it to the cell to the right of Grade. Now click on Grade and drag it to the upper left of the worksheet. The resulting pivot table should look like Figure 2.13.

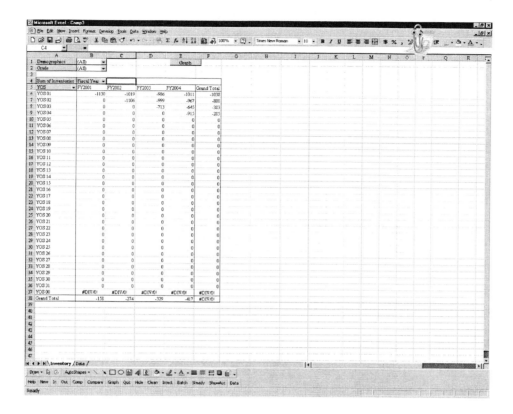

Figure 2.13—Modified Inventory Pivot Table

As noted above, the compare function in CAPM has a default setting that computes weighted averages of values. A weighted average is useful when comparing ACOL values and retention rates, but it does not always give realistic results when comparing grouped inventories (e.g., when inventories are displayed by FY). To get the "raw" numerical changes in personnel, right-click anywhere in the pivot table to display a pivot table dialogue box and select "Wizard." Then click on "Layout" to show pivot table display options. Next, click and drag Inventories (now in the center of the table) out of the table. Click on "Inventory0" and drag it into the pivot table. Click OK and Finish to return to the pivot table. After making these adjustments and changing the format of the cells to give integer values, the first few rows of the pivot table should look something like Figure 2.14.

Sum of Inventory0	Fiscal Year ▾				
YOS ▾	FY2001	FY2002	FY2003	FY2004	Grand Total
YOS 01	0	110	155	171	436
YOS 02	0	-110	-1	42	-69
YOS 03	0	0	-154	-49	-203
YOS 04	0	0	0	-163	-163

Figure 2.14—Net Changes from Increasing the Percentage of WML

The numbers in Figure 2.14 indicate that the change in aptitude requirements would not have much effect on the inventory in the first four years of service. However, we can get more insight into what is going on by clicking on the down arrow next to demographics in the upper-left corner of the worksheet and selecting "WMH" to see what has happened to the white male, high-aptitude population. The pivot table should look something like Figure 2.15.

Demographics	WMH ▾			Graph	
Grade	(All) ▾				
Sum of Inventory0	Fiscal Year ▾				
YOS ▾	FY2001	FY2002	FY2003	FY2004	Grand Total
YOS 01	-4347	-3990	-3891	-3997	-16225
YOS 02	0	-4056	-3722	-3630	-11408
YOS 03	0	0	-3806	-3492	-7298
YOS 04	0	0	0	-3571	-3571

Figure 2.15—Inventory Changes for WMH Personnel

As expected, the number of high-aptitude white male recruits is smaller than in the base case, and the lower recruitment level shows up in lower numbers of WMH personnel in future years. Figure 2.16 shows that further insight can be gained by restricting the pivot table to low-aptitude white males (WML).

Demographics	WML ▾			Graph	
Grade	(All) ▾				
Sum of Inventory0	Fiscal Year ▾				
YOS ▾	FY2001	FY2002	FY2003	FY2004	Grand Total
YOS 01	4380	4091	4021	4139	16631
YOS 02	0	3975	3713	3649	11338
YOS 03	0	0	3679	3436	7115
YOS 04	0	0	0	3433	3433

Figure 2.16—Inventory Changes for WML Personnel

The reductions in WMH recruits are just about matched by increases in WML recruits. However, the cumulative continuation rate over time appears to be higher for high-aptitude recruits than for low-aptitude recruits: By FY2004, there are 3,571 fewer WMH personnel in the YOS 4 inventory than in the base case, but there are only 3,433 more in the WML category.

Voluntary Loss Incentives

CAPM has been designed so that users can model "loss incentives" as special cases of a broader category of deferred compensation plans. When the models are run, CAPM evaluates the changes in the ACOL resulting from these plans and adjusts reenlistment rates accordingly. For the second exercise in this section, we will model the selective separation bonus (SSB) and Temporary Early Retirement Authority (TERA, the 15-year retirement option), both of which were programs used in the early 1990s to induce people to leave the service as part of the military force drawdown. The SSB allowed people to leave the military after five YOS with a lump-sum bonus that was 75 percent of their annual base pay. The amount increased by 15 percent for each YOS over five, so that an individual could leave after 14 YOS with a lump-sum bonus that was 210 percent of his or her base pay. TERA allowed people to retire before 20 YOS with annuities. After 15 YOS, the monthly value of the annuity was 35.625 percent of monthly base pay; after 19 YOS, the monthly value was 47.025 percent of monthly base pay.[10] We will demonstrate that CAPM can model the economic features of these programs with high fidelity. For this exercise, we will model the programs as though they were untargeted.[11]

Modifying the Model's Parameters to Reflect the Policy Change

To model this alternative case, open a new scenario by pressing New on the CAPM toolbar. Press Initialize and set the base year at 2000, the initial year at 2001, and the final year at 2005. Name this scenario "afhist3" or something similar. Click on Proceed.

---

[10]Retired pay for TERA is first calculated at 2.5 percent per YOS (like normal retirement pay) and then reduced by a factor that is 1/12th of 1 percent for each full month by which the person retires "early," that is, before completing 20 YOS. Thus, after 15 YOS, a person's retirement calculation yields $(15)(2.5\%) = 37.5\%$. Since the person is retiring five years, or 60 months, early, the reduction factor is $(60)(0.01/12) = 0.05$. The retirement multiple is thus $(1 - 0.05)(37.5\%) = (0.95)(37.5\%) = 35.625\%$.

[11]Section 4 discusses how to use CAPM to study the effects of policy changes on AFSCs at the three-digit level.

- Open the "Input: policies, parameters and data" area of the screen, then click on ⊞ next to "Retirement."

- In the matrix that appears, note the three columns that specify the three retirement systems currently in effect ("Pre-1981," "High3," and "Redux/High3"). To model SSB and TERA, we will add two new columns to this matrix. Fill in the rows of these two new columns as indicated in Figure 2.17, then click the cell containing Reset . Note that the three existing retirement plans, SSB, and TERA are specified so that they are orthogonal; that is, there are no situations in which an individual leaving the service would qualify for more than one program: Individuals are eligible for SSB from 5 to 14 YOS, for TERA from 15 to 19 YOS, and for full retirement after 20 YOS. The CAPM users' guide (MR-1668-AF/OSD) describes the matrix entries in more detail, but notice that under SSB the initial YOS multiplier is 75 percent and the "Max" YOS multiplier is 210 percent; these values help capture the structure of the program. Also note that for SSB, both the initial payment age and the final payment age are zero. CAPM interprets this to mean that the payment is a lump sum. For TERA, the initial payment age is zero, but the final payment age is 100. CAPM interprets this to mean that TERA is paid out as an annuity. After you have added the new columns, close the section by clicking on ⊟ next to Retirement .

- Click All models in the "Model run" box.

Reset					
Add Special Matrices	Pre-1981	High3	Redux/High3	SSB	TERA
First cohort	1900	1981	1987	1900	1900
Last cohort	1980	1986	2500	2005	2005
Vesting YOS	20	20	20	5	15
Last YOS	30	30	30	14	19
Initial YOS multiplier	50%	50%	40%	75%	35.63%
Max YOS multiplier	75%	75%	75%	210%	47.03%
Vesting grade	1	1	1	1	1
Cap grade	1	1	1	1	1
Initial grade multiplier	0%	0%	0%	0	0
Max grade Multiplier	0%	0%	0%	0	0
Overall max multiplier	75%	75%	75%	210%	47.03%
Initial payment age	0	0	0	0	0
Final payment age	100	100	100	0	100
Pay basis	0	1	1	0	0
Interest/COLA rate	5%	5%	5%	5%	5%
Continue after last YOS?	0	0	0	0	0
Special Pension Matrix					
Eligibility matrix					

NOTE: For those who entered military service before September 8, 1980, retirement pay is a multiple of final basic pay; the multiple is 2.5 percent times the YOS. For those who entered military service between September 8, 1980, and August 1, 1986, retirement pay is based on the average basic pay for the highest 36 months of the person's career (usually the average of his or her last three YOS). The Military Reform Act of 1986 created the REDUX retirement system (which, among other features, reduces the multiplier) and applied it to all members who joined on or after August 1, 1986. The National Defense Authorization Act for FY2000 made two major changes: (1) It allows those in this group to choose between the High-3 retirement system and the REDUX retirement system, and (2) it gives a $30,000 bonus to individuals who, at their 15th YOS, agree to stay in the military through at least 20 YOS and retire under the REDUX retirement system. See the military compensation web site maintained by OSD—http://dod.mil/militarypay, accessed April 2003. We will use the retirement plans as shown in this figure for illustrative purposes only.

Figure 2.17—SSB and TERA Specifications in the "Retirements" Matrix

Comparing the Results with the Baseline Case

A policy analyst might be interested in the long-term inventory effects of implementing the SSB and TERA options. An easy way to analyze these effects is to use the "Compare" function to compare inventories over time.

- Click on Compare to open the comparison dialogue box. Use "New – Old" as the method of comparison, and after pressing Proceed, select "afhist3" (or whatever you named the scenario with SSB/TERA) as the new file and "afhist1" (or whatever your "base" case was named) as the old file.

- Press ACOL. Manipulate the pivot table by dragging Fiscal Year from the page field to the column field and Grade from the column field to the page field so that the display is by YOS and FY. This will provide a sense of how the average ACOL in a given year of service has changed with the new retirement options. Your display should look something like Figure 2.18.

Sum of ACOLs	Fiscal Year ▼				
YOS ▼	FY2001	FY2002	FY2003	FY2004	Grand Total
YOS 01	$755	$755	$755	$755	$755
YOS 02	$1,573	$1,632	$1,632	$1,632	$1,620
YOS 03	$2,193	$2,193	$2,193	$2,193	$2,193
YOS 04	$2,578	$2,578	$2,578	$2,579	$2,578
YOS 05	-$1,264	-$1,266	-$1,265	-$1,265	-$1,265
YOS 06	-$1,835	-$1,838	-$1,838	-$1,838	-$1,837
YOS 07	-$2,393	-$2,391	-$2,372	-$2,371	-$2,382
YOS 08	-$2,774	-$2,767	-$2,755	-$2,733	-$2,757
YOS 09	-$1,822	-$1,830	-$1,830	-$1,828	-$1,827
YOS 10	-$424	-$444	-$456	-$471	-$448
YOS 11	$6,443	$6,441	$6,416	$6,398	$6,425
YOS 12	$5,520	$5,533	$5,529	$5,507	$5,522
YOS 13	$13,927	$13,952	$13,972	$13,969	$13,953
YOS 14	$36,269	$36,313	$36,367	$36,402	$36,333
YOS 15	-$14,420	-$14,542	-$14,599	-$14,628	-$14,537
YOS 16	-$28,402	-$21,888	-$21,966	-$22,005	-$24,010
YOS 17	-$59,167	-$59,259	-$48,376	-$48,540	-$54,748
YOS 18	-$108,712	-$108,663	-$108,680	-$87,952	-$104,263
YOS 19	-$286,318	-$285,671	-$285,375	-$285,286	-$285,656
YOS 20	$0	$0	$0	$0	$0

Figure 2.18—ACOL Changes Resulting from SSB/TERA

Interpreting the Results

Recall that ACOL is an expression of the difference in income a person will receive by staying in the Air Force until some future date and the income that would be received by leaving for a civilian job now. Notice that from YOS 01 through YOS 04 the difference in the cost of leaving between the SSB/TERA case and the base case is positive: The SSB/TERA plan makes it more lucrative to stay in the Air Force (the cost of leaving is higher). This indicates that people in these cohorts look ahead and see that it is to their advantage to stay in the Air Force until they are eligible for SSB or TERA. From YOS 05 through YOS 10, the changes in ACOL values induced by SSB (which can be received in those years) are negative, indicating that with the SSB/TERA scenario people benefit more by leaving the Air Force than they do in the base case, when SSB is not available.

From YOS 11 to YOS 14, the difference in ACOL values becomes positive again. Apparently, people in these cohorts calculate that the value of staying in the Air Force in order to receive early retirement benefits under TERA (which is available in YOS 15) outweighs the value of leaving immediately and receiving the SSB. From YOS 15 to YOS 19, the negative ACOL values indicate that, compared with the base case, it is more advantageous to leave the Air Force and take the benefits offered under TERA.

There are two important points to note when comparing ACOL values in this case. First, remember that CAPM presents the ACOL values as weighted averages, with the inventory in each cell as the weight. This means that if you look at the ACOL values in the SSB/TERA workbook and compare them with the ACOL values in the base case workbook, the numbers might be slightly different than what the "Compare" function calculates. This also means that you can get a slightly different picture of things if you look at ACOL values by demographic category or grade.

Second, the default CAPM setting for a reenlistment period is four years until YOS 14, after which reenlistments are assumed to be annual decisions. This means that when making ACOL calculations, CAPM will assume that if a person who is at four YOS does not leave now, the next time he can leave will be after eight total YOS. One consequence of this is that the value of staying will be averaged over the reenlistment period. For example, with SSB a person at four YOS sees the value of staying in service through five YOS; but if he stays in, he will not be able to leave again (according to the model) until he completes eight YOS. Thus, the model will really compare the value of leaving after *eight* YOS with the value of leaving after four. This means that any increased benefit from staying in the Air Force will be spread out (annualized) over that four-year period. If the SSB policy is supposed to allow people to leave without completing a reenlistment period, then, the model might understate the value of leaving. One way to experiment with this effect would be to see what happens if you change the reenlistment period to one year. This would allow a person to stay just one more year, receive the benefit, and leave.

Figure 2.18 also provides an example of how CAPM can pick up unexpected consequences of policy changes. Note that for those with 18 YOS, the introduction of the TERA option has a different effect in FY2004 than in earlier fiscal years: The magnitude of the ACOL change is about $20,000 lower (negative $87,952 as opposed to negative $109,680). Close examination of the way this example was constructed shows that starting in FY2004, individuals with 18 YOS are under the REDUX/High-3 retirement program, whose benefits are lower than those available under the "Pre-1981" or "High-3" plans. The change at 18 YOS in FY2004 is an indication that for this group of individuals, the potential effect of the introduction of the TERA option might be different and deserves closer attention.

24

We can look at the effect on inventories by using the graphing capability of the "Compare" function. Press the Data tab at the bottom of the "Compare" worksheet. This returns you to the sheet that allows you to select output options. Press Inventory , and manipulate the pivot table to display inventory by YOS and fiscal year.[12] Now press Graph at the top of the worksheet. CAPM will automatically produce a graphical display. The default graph is a bar graph, but by using ordinary Excel graph options, you can easily change the chart type to get the "ribbon" graph shown in Figure 2.19.

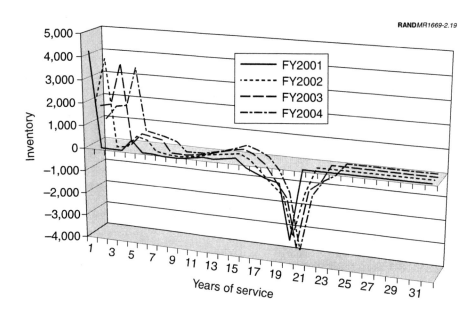

Figure 2.19—Inventory Changes Resulting from SSB/TERA

In the graph, notice that in the first fiscal year of the projection, the inventory at 5 YOS is larger than it was in the base case.[13] This makes sense because more people who would originally have left after 4 YOS will now stay through at least 5 YOS in order to take advantage of the SSB option. From YOS 6 through YOS 11, some people are induced to leave, but compared to the overall Air Force population, the number is relatively small. The inventory at YOS 15 is larger than in the base case because people will want to complete at least 15 YOS in order to receive the TERA option. From YOS 16 to YOS 20, we see a significant decrease in inventory: The value of the early retirement option is enough to encourage people to leave. Note that in the first projection year, the inventory at

---

[12]As noted earlier, inventory changes are best examined by changing the pivot table so that Inventory0 values are used.

[13]Looking at the inventory pivot table can make it easier to see the actual values that the model calculates for each year.

21 YOS has not changed. This is because the TERA option did not affect the value of retirement for those who complete 20 YOS. Finally, notice that the inventory in the first YOS has increased, since CAPM calculates the need for more accessions because of the people who were induced to leave.

Notice that the humps at YOS one and YOS five in the first projection year advance in following projection years. Because accessions were higher in FY2001, the inventory in YOS two is larger than the base case in FY2002. Similarly, the increase in inventory at five YOS in FY2001 has consequences for the inventory at YOS six, seven, and eight for FYs 2002, 2003, and 2004, respectively. The losses induced in FY2001 also have consequences for follow-on projection years. The departure of a large number of people at YOS 20 in FY2001 means that the YOS 21 inventory in FY2002 is smaller.

Consequences of the SSB/TERA options can be examined much more closely by checking ACOLs and inventories by grade.

3. Compensation

The policy issues explored in this section include changes in the basic pay table, a targeted bonus, and modifying the cost of living adjustment (COLA) for retired pay. The pay exercise will check for different effects of the January 2001 pay table (the default pay table in CAPM 2.2) compared with the January 2000 pay table. The second exercise provides background on CAPM calculations in order to explain how to input targeted bonuses, and the third explores the implications of a cap on retired pay increases at 1 percent less than inflation.

New Pay Tables

The framework for using CAPM to test the retention, inventory, and cost effects of a new pay table is the same as for previous exercises, but the first stage this time is to prepare a new pay table.[1]

Preparing a Pay Table Spreadsheet[2]

The 2001 pay tables used by CAPM 2.2 are contained in the Policy.db file located in the Data subdirectory.[3] The basic pay table is the first entry in this file, starting at cell A1. RMC starts in cell A67.[4] RMC is used by CAPM for an individual's income in the service; the basic pay is needed to calculate retirement income. To run the alternative analysis, a spreadsheet containing new pay tables must also be constructed.

---

[1] A model incorporating pay grade (as CAPM does) is required in order to evaluate pay table issues. A pay grade dimension and its accompanying promotion routines add much complexity to a model, but significantly increase the range of policies that can be evaluated.

[2] This exercise will produce a file containing January 2000 pay tables. Readers who are comfortable with manipulating Excel spreadsheets can skip this exercise part and use January 2000 pay tables in the Payalt.db file (located in the Data subfolder of the CAPM folder).

[3] CAPM 2.2 has a very helpful feature that allows the user to inspect the data used by the model. The CAPM toolbar has a button labeled Data . Pressing this button displays a dialogue box that lists all named data items in the model. If "basic pay" is selected, pressing Inspect will open the worksheet in which basic pay data are stored and highlight the data range associated with the data name.

[4] RMC includes basic pay, basic allowance for subsistence, housing allowance, and the imputed tax advantage from tax-free allowances. RMC is only approximate; the values included in CAPM are based on the *2001 Uniformed Services Almanac*.

A convenient way to prepare the alternative spreadsheet is to copy the basic pay (cells B1–K32, including row and column headings) and RMC tables (cells B67–K98, including row and column headings) from Policy.db and paste them into a new spreadsheet—one in cells A1–J32 and one in cells L1–U32. Skip a row and paste another copy of the original tables below the first copy (this will put the second copy of the tables in rows 34 through 65). The new spreadsheet may be named, for example, "Payalt.db" and stored in the Data subdirectory. (Note: To ensure that Excel saves the file as an *.db file, you must type in quotation marks as part of the name. For example, if you type in Payalt.db without the quotation marks, Excel will save the file as Payalt.db.xls.) Now key the data from the January pay tables shown in Appendix A into the second set of pasted matrices in Payalt.db.[5] Note that in the spreadsheet matrix rows correspond to YOS, and the columns correspond to grade, unlike published pay tables, which are the other way around. You should now have the original CAPM basic pay and RMC tables in rows 1 through 32, and the January 2000 tables in rows 34 through 65.

Since CAPM uses annual basic pay and RMC, the monthly basic pay table must now be adjusted.

- Copy both matrices in Payalt.db into which you have just keyed the new data, then skip a line or two below them and paste them.

- Replace the contents of the E1/YOS 1 cell in the basic pay pasted matrix (B69 or something close to it) with "=B36*12." This assumes B36 is the E1/YOS 1 cell in your original January matrix.

- Copy the cell across to the E9 column, then copy this row down to the YOS 30 row. Since the RMC table in the Appendix is already in annual terms, you do not need to make any adjustment.

- Later, we will instruct CAPM to use these new matrices rather than the standard pay table matrix. To make it easy to point CAPM toward the alternative matrices, it is useful to give them a range name, such as Jan_basic_pay and Jan_RMC. To do this, highlight the annual basic pay matrix (the data only, not row and column headings). On the Excel toolbar, click on $\boxed{\text{Insert}}$, then $\boxed{\text{Name}}$, then $\boxed{\text{Define}}$. A dialogue box will appear. In the "Name:" box, type "Jan_basic_pay" (including the underscore). The "Refers to:" box will already contain "=$B69:$J$98" or whatever range you have highlighted. Click $\boxed{\text{OK}}$. Do the same for the RMC pay table.

---

[5]Note also that the basic pay table is monthly pay; the RMC table is *annual* pay.

In the interpretation stage of this analysis, you might be interested in observing how the new pay tables differ from the CAPM default tables. To do this, copy the January basic pay table and paste it below the existing January pay table (this will put it in cells A100:J132, or close to them). Replace each cell with the difference between the January 2000 pay table and the original CAPM pay table. For example, the E1/YOS 1 cell, which is probably B103 or something close to it, might contain "=B36-B3" if you are comparing monthly pay (you could use "=B69-12*B3" to compare annual pay). Once the formula is correctly entered in the cell, it can be copied across and down to fill the matrix.

Defining the Baseline Case

The first step in studying the changes induced by the new pay table is to initialize a baseline scenario:

- From the CAPM screen, open a new scenario sheet by clicking New in the toolbar at the bottom of the screen.

- In the scenario sheet that appears, click on Initialize Data. In the initialization dialogue box, use USAF as the service, leave 2000 as the base year, and set the begin and end years at 2001 and 2004, respectively. Type in "Baseline" or something similar for the label.[6] This dialogue box also allows you to choose how the model will calculate reenlistment rates from the ACOL values. Select "ACOL II coefficients" and "Delta method." Click on Proceed to complete this part of the setup.

- The default parameters supplied by CAPM are drawn from the annual personnel plans submitted by the services to the Office of the Under Secretary of Defense (Personnel and Readiness) or from other standard sources.[7] The baseline case requires no changes to policy parameters.

- Click All models in the "Model run" box.

After the run is completed, the name of the input file automatically changes to "Baseline.out."

---

[6]If you have done the exercises from Section 2, you can use afhist1.out as your base case.

[7]The default policy parameters are not static throughout all future years—they will capture known policy changes reflected in the service plans. Thus, a baseline scenario run using the default parameters represents "policies as currently planned" rather than "constant policies."

Modifying the Model's Parameters

To develop scenarios with the new pay tables, start from the CAPM screen again and initialize a new scenario using a label such as "testalt1" for the January 2000 pay table. Use the same service and projected years as the baseline scenario. The only change required in the policy parameters is to instruct the model to use the new pay tables:

- Click $\boxed{+}$ next to "Input: policies, parameters and data," then open the "Compensation, reenlistment" cell. Finally, click $\boxed{+}$ next to "Compensation elements."

- You will see a cell in the resulting table labeled "Basic pay." Immediately to the right in a column headed "Source" is a cell containing a pointer to the pay table matrix used by the model. The default parameter will read as follows: "'\CAPM\data\policy.db'!basic_pay," or some variation of this if you are not using the standard CAPM directory and subdirectories. In the previous stage, you created a file named Payalt.db containing pay ranges named Jan_basic_pay and Jan_RMC. To use the January basic pay table, click on the cell with the default parameter and edit it to read "'\CAPM\data\payalt.db'!Jan_basic_pay."

- The cell below "Basic pay" is labeled "RMC." The pointer for RMC must be changed just as the basic pay pointer was. Click on the cell with the default location and edit it to read "'\CAPM\data\payalt.db'!Jan_RMC." You can now click the minus signs to the left of "Compensation elements," "Compensation," and "Policies" if you desire to clean up the screen.

- Click $\boxed{\text{All models}}$.

Comparing the Results of the Two Runs

Use CAPM's "Compare" function to compare the two scenarios:

- Click on $\boxed{\text{Compare}}$ on the CAPM toolbar at the bottom of the screen. The "Comparison" screen will appear.

- If you wish to save this file, keep the "Automatically Save Results" box checked; otherwise, you can uncheck it.

- Select the "New – Old" option in the "Basis for comparison" section.

- Leave the "Inventory for ACOL, Re-enlistment pivot tables" selection as "Average."

30

- Select the "Single pair of cases" option. If that option is already selected, click $\boxed{\text{Proceed}}$.

- A dialogue box will appear asking you to select the $\boxed{\text{New}}$ case file. Since we want to see the effect of the pay increase, select Baseline.out or whatever label you used for the baseline scenario.

- The next dialogue box will ask you to select the $\boxed{\text{Old}}$ case file. Select *testalt1.out* or whatever label you used for the January 2000 pay table case.

The program will now prepare a workbook named "CompX" (X means this is the Xth comparison sheet prepared in this session) comparing the two cases.

Interpreting the Results

A quick glance at the pay tables shows that pay increased in all pay grades. Obviously, one of the objectives of the new pay table is to increase overall retention in the Air Force, and we would expect ACOL values, and through them retention rates, to roughly follow these increases. $\boxed{\text{ETS continuation rates}}$ on the comparison sheet opens the pivot table of reenlistment rates, and Figure 3.1 shows a graph of the changes in rates as calculated by CAPM.

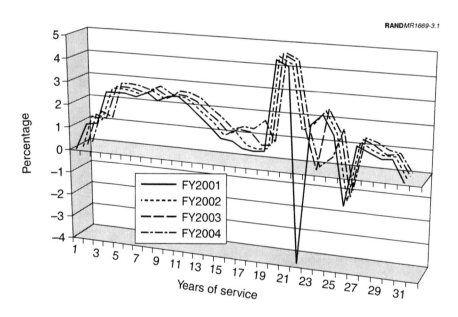

Figure 3.1—Reenlistment Rate Changes Based on January 2000 Pay Tables

This figure shows the change in percentage of those at ETS who reenlist. This display is a weighted average of the changes for different grades; more insight can be gained by looking at individual grades or at the change in inventory that results from the pay table change. As expected, the increase in pay increases the retention rate in most YOS. What might come as a surprise initially is that the retention rates after YOS 20 decrease in some cases. Remember that the increase in *basic* pay means that *retirement pay* increases; thus there are cases in which the retirement pay increase under the 2001 pay table is enough to induce more people to retire.

This is especially noticeable in the FY2001 projection year in Figure 3.1. Under the retirement plans used in this example, the retirement pay in FY2001 for those with 22 YOS is based on final basic pay. In later projection years, those with 22 YOS are under the High-3 plan. The large decrease in retention for those at YOS 22 in FY2001 shows that the increase in final pay resulting from the new pay table increases the retirement benefit enough to overcome the increase in pay for staying. In later projection years under the High-3 plan, this is not the case.

A Targeted Bonus

The second exercise in the compensation area involves simulating the effects of a targeted bonus on inventory changes. CAPM allows you to create a special pay matrix of bonuses that can target populations by grade and YOS. For this exercise, we assume that the Air Force is concerned that not enough E4s are reenlisting after completing eight YOS. To induce more people in this cohort to reenlist, the Air Force decides to offer a reenlistment bonus of $20,000.

Creating a Bonus Pay Table

To study the effects of a targeted bonus, we must create a pay matrix that provides the bonus payment.

- Copy the basic pay table (including row and column headings) from the Policy.db file and paste it into a new spreadsheet. Use Payalt.db from the last exercise if you wish.

- Select all pay values in the matrix and delete them. Then replace all of the values with zero *except* the values for E4s and E5s at nine YOS. In these positions, put 20,000. A person who makes the decision to reenlist after completing eight YOS will only receive the bonus if he stays in for the ninth year; that is why the bonus must go in the YOS nine position. When calculating ACOL values, CAPM considers the probability that a person will be promoted to the next higher grade. Thus, an E4 at YOS eight who is considering staying will note the possibility of being either an E4 or an E5 at nine YOS. For this reason, even though we are targeting only E4s at eight YOS, the bonus matrix must have the bonus amount for both E4s and E5s at YOS nine.

- Select the values in the pay table (not including row and column headings). Select "Insert," "Name," and "Define." In the dialogue box that appears, type "E4_Bonus_Pay" to name the pay table.

Modifying the Model's Parameters

Now you can set up the scenario sheet for this problem.

- Click New on the CAPM menu bar to open a new scenario sheet.
- Click Initialize Data to open up the initialization dialogue box. Name the scenario "E4_Bonus" or something similar. Use 2000 as the base year, 2001 as the initial projection year, and 2004 as the final projection year. Click Proceed.
- To take the bonus into account, we must adjust the compensation elements of the scenario sheet. As with the previous exercise, click + next to "Input: policies, parameters and data," then open the "Compensation, reenlistment" cell. Finally, click + next to "Compensation elements."
- Click in the "Civilian pay" cell (this helps ensure that the bonus is entered properly), then click on Add Row that is below the "Civilian pay" cell. A dialogue box called "New Pay Element" should appear. In the "Name" section of the dialogue box, you can write "E4 Bonus." Then in the "Pay Type" section, click next to number 5 for reenlistment bonus. Click Add Pay Element and the dialogue box will disappear. You will now see that a new row has been added in the compensation elements section, and it is called "E4 Bonus."
- Now that the new row has been added, CAPM must be told where to find the new pay element. As with the alternate pay tables in the previous exercise, this information is added in the "Source Column." In this case, the source will be "'\CAPM\data\payalt.db'!E4_Bonus_Pay" if you named the bonus pay table as suggested above.
- Click on All models to produce projected inventories.

Comparing the Two Runs and Interpreting the Results

To see how the bonus affects people, click on [Compare], use "E4 Bonus Pay.out" as the new file, and "Baseline.out" (or whatever you named your base case) as the old file. Open the "Outputs" section of the worksheet, and click on ACOLs. Click on the arrow next to the Fiscal Year button at the top of the page, and select 2001. Your pivot table should look something like Figure 3.2.

Sum of ACOLs	Grade ▼						
YOS ▼	E1-3	E4	E5	E6	E7	E8	E9
YOS 01	$0	#DIV/0!	#DIV/0!	#DIV/0!	#DIV/0!	#DIV/0!	#DIV/0!
YOS 02	$0	$0	$0	$0	#DIV/0!	#DIV/0!	#DIV/0!
YOS 03	$0	$0	$0	$0	#DIV/0!	#DIV/0!	#DIV/0!
YOS 04	$1,444	$1,212	$524	$0	#DIV/0!	#DIV/0!	#DIV/0!
YOS 05	$0	$0	$0	$0	$0	#DIV/0!	#DIV/0!
YOS 06	$0	$0	$0	$0	#DIV/0!	#DIV/0!	$0
YOS 07	$0	$0	$0	$0	$0	#DIV/0!	#DIV/0!
YOS 08	$4,585	$6,114	$6,053	$0	$0	$0	#DIV/0!
YOS 09	$0	$0	$0	$0	$0	#DIV/0!	#DIV/0!

Figure 3.2—ACOL Changes from a Targeted E4 Bonus

Remember that since the default setting for the Compare function is to calculate weighted averages of ACOL values, the #Div/0! values in the table mean that there are no enlisted personnel in those cells.

The table shows that the cost of leaving after 8 YOS for an E4 has increased, because it will mean giving up the bonus. What may come as a surprise is that the cost of leaving did not increase by the $20,000 value of the bonus. The reason for this is that CAPM assumes that individuals enlist for four-year periods.[8] Thus, if an individual reenlists after eight YOS, he or she cannot leave for another four years. Computationally, this means that CAPM will not base the ACOL value on the possibility of leaving after nine YOS (and after pocketing the $20,000). The model will compute the value of staying through YOS 12 and compare that with the value of leaving now. This means that the value of the $20,000 bonus is spread out over a few years so that the *annualized* value is less than the bonus itself.

Because of the construction of the bonus pay table, Figure 3.2 also shows that E3s at eight YOS will see an ACOL increase (because they have a chance of being

[8]This is the default setting. After 14 YOS, reenlistment decisions can be made annually. Both of these settings can be modified in the scenario sheet.

promoted to E4), and E5s do, too (because they have a chance of remaining in grade E5). Figure 3.2 also indicates that individuals at four YOS will feel the effect of the bonus. This is because of CAPM's four-year enlistment period default: A person who reenlists after four YOS will not be able leave before completing eight YOS, and CAPM's ACOL calculations will pick up the bonus that the person must consider giving up if he or she leaves at that time.

Figure 3.3 shows the effect of the targeted bonus on E5 inventories over time.[9] CAPM predicts that after the first year of the E4 targeted bonus, there will be more E5s in the inventory in YOS nine. The effect of the bonus at YOS nine decreases as we move into the future, partly because one consequence of the better retention in 2001 is that fewer people will need to be recruited, so there will be fewer people moving up in the ranks after 2001. Note also that the model predicts that the inventory at YOS five will also increase slightly. The model calculates that these individuals, who are at their first reenlistment opportunity, will be influenced to stay because of the possibility of a bonus at their *second* opportunity.

Sum of Inventory0	Fiscal Year ▾			
YOS ▾	FY2001	FY2002	FY2003	FY2004
YOS 01	0	0	0	0
YOS 02	0	0	0	0
YOS 03	0	0	0	0
YOS 04	0	0	0	-1
YOS 05	14	14	15	15
YOS 06	0	51	51	53
YOS 07	0	0	99	101
YOS 08	0	0	0	130
YOS 09	150	138	143	145
YOS 10	0	136	124	127
YOS 11	0	0	118	107
YOS 12	0	0	0	101

Figure 3.3—E5 Inventory Changes Caused by an E4 Bonus

A COLA Cap for Retired Pay

The third exercise in the compensation area involves simulating the effects of the so-called Diet COLA—capping retired pay COLAs at the level of employment-

---

[9]As noted earlier, inventory changes are best examined by changing the pivot table so that Inventory0 values are used.

cost-index increases minus one percentage point. Since a COLA cap will reduce the present value of the retired pay element of the returns to staying in military service, Diet COLA will generally reduce ACOLs and therefore reduce retention.

Developing the Scenarios

Setting up this exercise requires some manipulation, because CAPM 2.2 allows the user a lot of flexibility in adjusting important parameters. The three most important parameters in this case are the interest rate, the retirement pay interest rate, and the inflation rate.

The interest rate is set in the "General" section of the scenario sheet. This rate is used in calculating costs, but by default it is also used as the discount rate to calculate the present value of the income stream from retirement pay. If you open the "Retirement" section of the scenario sheet, you will see that the row labeled "Interest/COLA Rate" has the same value as the interest rate in the "General" section. The inflation rate is set in the "Constraints" section, in row 155 of the scenario sheet; this rate can be set to different values for different projection years. The inflation rate is used in CAPM to evaluate the present value of future decisions. For example, for a person at 15 YOS considering the value of waiting until 20 YOS to leave the Air Force, CAPM will use the retirement interest rate to calculate the present value (at 20 YOS) of the retirement income stream. Then it will use the inflation rate to calculate the present value at 15 YOS of the income stream that will start at 20 YOS.

Setting up a baseline scenario for this exercise is done just as in previous exercises. The baseline scenario will use default parameter values; the steps below will just remind you of where things are located.

- Open a new scenario sheet by clicking ⟦New⟧ on the toolbar at the bottom of any screen.
- Click ⟦Initialize Data⟧ on the scenario sheet. In the dialogue box that appears, enter a label such as "Diet Baseline." Select USAF as the service, accept 2000 as the base year, enter 2001 as the initial year, and enter 2004 as the final year.
- Open the "Input: policies, parameters and data" area, then the "Constraints" area. In the Constraints screen, you will find a matrix with policy and environmental parameters listed on the left and the projected years over which the model will run listed across the top. Find the row labeled "Inflation" and the six rows immediately beneath it, which are labeled "Basic Pay COLA" through "Retirement COLA." The default value for the inflation

rate is 5.3 percent. Leave this value as it is. The COLA rows are inactive in the CAPM 2.2 release. You can clean up the screen by clicking on ⊟ next to "Constraints."

- Still in the "Input: policies, parameters and data" area, click ⊞ next to General. In the General screen, click the cell marked "Interest rate." This is the rate used to discount all projected regular military compensation and accession costs in CAPM's cost outputs.[10] The default interest rate is 5 percent; leave this value as it is.

- Click next to the "Retirement" cell. In the Retirement screen, you will find a matrix containing parameters for each of the three retirement plans currently in effect. Locate the row labeled "Interest/COLA rate" and note that, as mentioned above, this rate is already set to the interest rate of 5 percent for each of the three plans. These rates are used to discount the cost of retirement in CAPM's cost outputs, but they are also used in discounting future retirement income.

- Click All models.

Modifying the Parameters

To run the alternative ("Diet COLA") case, take the following steps:

- Open a new scenario sheet and label it "Diet COLA." Open the "Input: policies, parameters and data" area.

- Click on ⊞ next to the "Retirement" cell to open the retirement plans.

- Locate the row labeled "Interest/COLA rate" and change the values under each retirement plan to 6 percent. Click Reset. This change in setting means that the present value of the retirement income stream will be discounted as if inflation were 6 percent instead of 5 percent.

- Click All models.

Comparing Outputs

- Click on Compare.

---

[10]CAPM reports the present value of all costs, discounted at the rates supplied here. Note that cost outputs are computed independently of ACOLs.

- At the "Comparison" screen, click $\boxed{\text{Automatically Save Results?}}$. In the space provided, type in a label for the workbook, such as "Diet1."[11]
- Select the "New – Old" option and the "Single pair of cases" option.
- Click $\boxed{\text{Proceed}}$.
- In the dialogue boxes that appear, select *Diet COLA.out* and *Diet Baseline.out* as the new and old cases, respectively.

First take a look at the effect of the reduced COLA on ACOL values by pressing $\boxed{\text{ACOL}}$. Figure 3.4 shows the result graphically, with the data arranged by YOS and fiscal year.

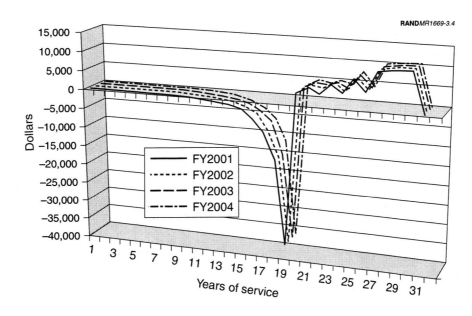

Figure 3.4—ACOL Changes from a COLA Cap

There is little effect on ACOL values until YOS 16, when the figure shows that the cost of leaving under the COLA cap is less than that without the cap. This situation continues through YOS 19. This makes sense because with the cap, the value of retirement pay decreases, so the value of remaining in the Air Force to earn retirement pay declines and the cost of leaving decreases. After YOS 20, however, the model indicates that the cost of leaving is greater under the COLA cap than without it. Without the COLA cap, a person who retires after 20 YOS receives a certain amount of retirement pay. With the COLA cap, the value of that retirement pay declines. Thus, with the cap, the value of leaving after 20

---

[11]CAPM will automatically add an .xlw workbook suffix to this label.

YOS is lower than that without the cap and the cost of leaving is greater. The model's calculations show that in the scenario with the cap, an individual gains more by staying in the military a little longer because he or she will earn more years of military pay and the value of retirement pay will also increase.

Figure 3.5 shows the effects of these changes on inventories from 15–25 YOS.[12] CAPM calculates that the loss in value of retirement pay has an effect on the decision to leave both before and after 20 YOS have been completed.

YOS	FY2001	FY2002	FY2003	FY2004
YOS 15	-18	-24	-32	-35
YOS 16	-22	-35	-36	-45
YOS 17	-34	-56	-63	-57
YOS 18	-25	-59	-85	-88
YOS 19	-23	-51	-85	-133
YOS 20	-181	-173	-217	-251
YOS 21	181	96	78	74
YOS 22	80	226	156	135
YOS 23	27	94	202	148
YOS 24	61	80	117	206
YOS 25	20	39	42	56

Figure 3.5—Inventory Effect of a COLA Cap

---

[12]As noted earlier, inventory changes are best examined by changing the pivot table so that Inventory0 values are used.

4. Disaggregate and Steady-State Scenarios

CAPM 2.2 has the capability to model Air Force inventories by three-digit AFSC. It can also calculate steady-state inventories: inventories that would result in the long run if current retention and promotion rates continued. Both types of analysis are simple to perform with built-in CAPM functions.

Disaggregate Scenarios

Disaggregate scenarios require only a few steps in addition to those used in any aggregate analysis. For this example, we will simply develop a "base case" scenario for the 2A1 (avionics) career field.

- From the CAPM screen, open a new scenario by pressing New.

- Press Initialize Data, set the initial year to 2001 and the final year to 2004, and name the scenario Test_2A1. Press Proceed.

- When the scenario sheet is initialized, you will notice a block at the top of the screen labeled "Disaggregate Data Section." This is shown in the left part of Figure 4.1; no doubt you have noticed this in the examples presented earlier in this tutorial. Press the only button in this block, labeled Build New 3-Digit Disaggregate File.

- After a few seconds, a dialogue box will appear that asks you to input a three-digit AFSC. This dialogue is shown in the right part of Figure 4.1. In the dialogue box, type in 2A1 and then press OK. The other selections in the dialogue box allow you to use reenlistment eligibility rates, reenlistment rates, and non-ETS continuation rates that will be calculated for the population in the new file. Since some of the cell populations for individual AFSCs are very small, this dialogue box also allows you to set default rates if the cells have no one in them. Because you made no inputs in the "warning" section for this exercise, CAPM will use the rate values for the entire enlisted population that are found in the USAF.dbg file.

- CAPM will perform a sort on the disaggregate source file and will produce a new file called 2A1.dbg. After it does so, it should send you back to the "Test_2A1" scenario sheet. If it does not, you can return to that sheet by clicking Window on the Excel toolbar and selecting "Test_2A1."

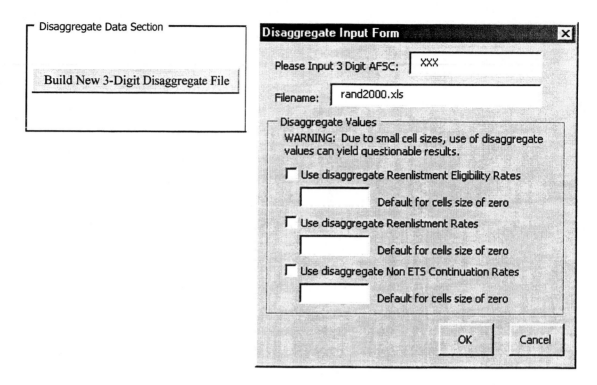

Figure 4.1—Disaggregate Dialogue Boxes

This process has done two things. First, it has created a new source file called 2A1.dbg that contains data for the selected three-digit AFSC. Second, it has changed some of the pointers in the scenario sheet so that CAPM uses the correct source information when the model is run. For example, if you open the "Input: policies, parameters and data" section and then open the "Personnel" section, you will see that the cell next to "Starting Inventory Source" now contains something like Capm\Data**2A1.dbg**'!VSINV. This shows that the data source is now the file 2A1.dbg, instead of USAF.dbg, which is the source during an aggregate run.

The effect of policy adjustments on this AFSC can now be studied in the same way as with the aggregate population. The disaggregate step merely sets up the proper data source for inventory, promotion, and continuation data.

Steady-State Runs

An analyst is often interested in the long-term consequences of a policy change; CAPM's steady-state function provides an easy way to study them. This function calculates what the force would look like if, over the long run, accessions, promotion rates, retention rates, and retirement rates remain the same, with the result that the force "settles down" and does not change from year to year. We will start this exercise by producing the steady-state inventory that results from CAPM's default data.

- Open a new scenario sheet and initialize it using 2000 as the initial year and 2000 as the final year. This input has no real effect on the steady-state scenario, since the steady-state computation does not produce any projection years. The scenario sheet in this case serves only to set up the sources of data for the steady-state calculation. Name the sheet "Test_ss" and press Proceed .
- Press the button labeled Steady on the CAPM toolbar at the bottom of the screen. The complicated-looking dialogue box titled "Steady State ("Objective") Force," shown in Figure 4.2, will appear. Ignore the details in the dialogue box for now, and press Compute Steady State Force .

After you press the button, CAPM will produce a workbook named "USAF.ss," as in Figure 4.3. The steady-state population, by YOS and grade, will be displayed in a pivot table located in cells H3–P37. The raw data for the pivot table is displayed in columns A through F. Additionally, the workbook contains a sheet labeled "Data." The data sheet lists the input information that was used to calculate the steady-state force.

A policy change that affects compensation might change reenlistment rates; a policy change that affects inventory limits by grade might require changes in promotion rates. Either change can have long-term effects on inventories, and the steady-state function provides a way to study these effects. Since the steady-state function uses input information from the scenario sheet, all that needs to be done to study the long-term effects of changes is to change the sources of information. The easiest way to do this is to change the appropriate information (promotion rates, for example) in the USAF.dbg file. When the steady-state function is used, it will automatically get data from the USAF.dbg file.

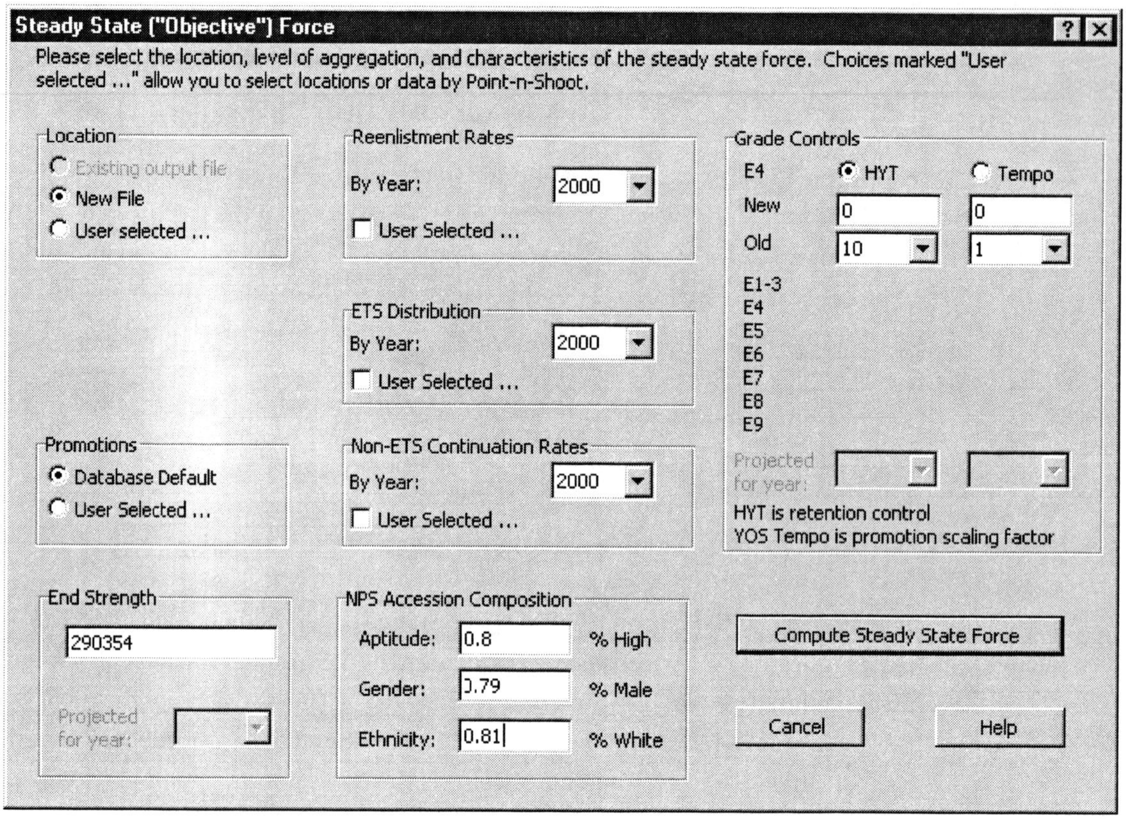

Figure 4.2—Steady-State Dialogue Box

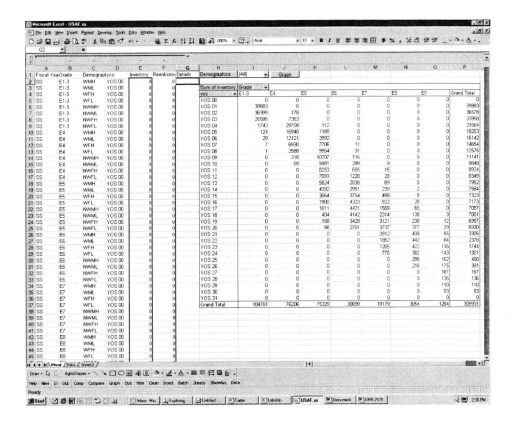

Figure 4.3—Steady-State Workbook

Appendix

January 2000 Pay Tables

Table A.1

January 2000 Monthly Basic Pay

Basic Pay YOS\GRADE	Monthly E1	E2	E3	E4	E5	E6	E7	E8	E9
1	930.00	1,127.40	1,171.50	1,242.90	1,332.60	1,518.90	1,765.80	0.00	0.00
2	1,005.60	1,127.40	1,235.70	1,312.80	1,450.50	1,655.70	1,906.20	0.00	0.00
3	1,005.60	1,127.40	1,284.60	1,390.20	1,521.00	1,724.40	1,976.10	0.00	0.00
4	1,005.60	1,127.40	1,335.90	1,497.30	1,587.30	1,797.60	2,045.70	0.00	0.00
5	1,005.60	1,127.40	1,335.90	1,497.30	1,587.30	1,797.60	2,045.70	0.00	0.00
6	1,005.60	1,127.40	1,335.90	1,556.70	1,691.70	1,865.40	2,115.60	0.00	0.00
7	1,005.60	1,127.40	1,335.90	1,556.70	1,691.70	1,865.40	2,115.60	0.00	0.00
8	1,005.60	1,127.40	1,335.90	1,556.70	1,761.00	1,932.60	2,182.80	2,528.40	0.00
9	1,005.60	1,127.40	1,335.90	1,556.70	1,761.00	1,932.60	2,182.80	2,528.40	0.00
10	1,005.60	1,127.40	1,335.90	1,556.70	1,830.00	2,003.40	2,252.70	2,601.60	3,015.30
11	1,005.60	1,127.40	1,335.90	1,556.70	1,830.00	2,003.40	2,252.70	2,601.60	3,015.30
12	1,005.60	1,127.40	1,335.90	1,556.70	1,898.10	2,106.60	2,323.20	2,669.70	3,083.40
13	1,005.60	1,127.40	1,335.90	1,556.70	1,898.10	2,106.60	2,323.20	2,669.70	3,083.40
14	1,005.60	1,127.40	1,335.90	1,556.70	1,932.60	2,172.90	2,427.90	2,739.00	3,152.70
15	1,005.60	1,127.40	1,335.90	1,556.70	1,932.60	2,172.90	2,427.90	2,739.00	3,152.70
16	1,005.60	1,127.40	1,335.90	1,556.70	1,932.60	2,242.80	2,496.90	2,811.60	3,225.60
17	1,005.60	1,127.40	1,335.90	1,556.70	1,932.60	2,242.80	2,496.90	2,811.60	3,225.60
18	1,005.60	1,127.40	1,335.90	1,556.70	1,932.60	2,277.00	2,566.20	2,875.50	3,298.20
19	1,005.60	1,127.40	1,335.90	1,556.70	1,932.60	2,277.00	2,566.20	2,875.50	3,298.20
20	1,005.60	1,127.40	1,335.90	1,556.70	1,932.60	2,277.00	2,599.50	2,946.30	3,361.50
21	1,005.60	1,127.40	1,335.90	1,556.70	1,932.60	2,277.00	2,599.50	2,946.30	3,361.50
22	1,005.60	1,127.40	1,335.90	1,556.70	1,932.60	2,277.00	2,774.40	3,119.40	3,537.90
23	1,005.60	1,127.40	1,335.90	1,556.70	1,932.60	2,277.00	2,774.40	3,119.40	3,537.90
24	1,005.60	1,127.40	1,335.90	1,556.70	1,932.60	2,277.00	2,912.40	3,258.00	3,675.60
25	1,005.60	1,127.40	1,335.90	1,556.70	1,932.60	2,277.00	2,912.40	3,258.00	3,675.60
26	1,005.60	1,127.40	1,335.90	1,556.70	1,932.60	2,277.00	3,119.40	3,467.10	3,882.60
27	1,005.60	1,127.40	1,335.90	1,556.70	1,932.60	2,277.00	3,119.40	3,467.10	3,882.60
28	1,005.60	1,127.40	1,335.90	1,556.70	1,932.60	2,277.00	3,119.40	3,467.10	3,882.60
29	1,005.60	1,127.40	1,335.90	1,556.70	1,932.60	2,277.00	3,119.40	3,467.10	3,882.60
30	1,005.60	1,127.40	1,335.90	1,556.70	1,932.60	2,277.00	3,119.40	3,467.10	3,882.60

SOURCE: *2000 Uniformed Services Almanac.*

Table A.2

January 2000 Annual RMC (estimated)

RMC YOS\GRADE	Annual E1	E2	E3	E4	E5	E6	E7	E8	E9
1	$21,848	$23,666	$24,140	$25,392	$27,949	$31,575	$38,633	$46,249	$54,130
2	$21,848	$23,666	$24,928	$26,270	$29,428	$33,131	$38,633	$46,249	$54,130
3	$21,848	$23,666	$24,928	$26,270	$29,428	$33,131	$38,633	$46,249	$54,130
4	$21,848	$23,666	$25,528	$27,197	$30,330	$33,984	$38,633	$46,249	$54,130
5	$21,848	$23,666	$26,153	$28,485	$31,112	$34,887	$38,633	$46,249	$54,130
6	$21,848	$23,666	$26,153	$28,485	$31,112	$34,887	$38,633	$46,249	$54,130
7	$21,848	$23,666	$26,153	$29,212	$32,301	$35,719	$39,488	$46,249	$54,130
8	$21,848	$23,666	$26,153	$29,212	$32,301	$35,719	$39,788	$46,249	$54,130
9	$21,848	$23,666	$26,153	$29,212	$33,127	$36,553	$40,309	$46,249	$54,130
10	$21,848	$23,666	$26,153	$29,212	$33,127	$36,553	$40,309	$46,249	$54,130
11	$21,848	$23,666	$26,153	$29,212	$33,962	$37,432	$41,163	$46,249	$54,130
12	$21,848	$23,666	$26,153	$29,212	$33,962	$37,432	$41,163	$46,249	$54,130
13	$21,848	$23,666	$26,153	$29,212	$34,799	$38,702	$42,025	$47,079	$54,130
14	$21,848	$23,666	$26,153	$29,212	$34,799	$38,702	$42,025	$47,079	$54,130
15	$21,848	$23,666	$26,153	$29,212	$35,236	$39,517	$43,304	$47,923	$54,130
16	$21,848	$23,666	$26,153	$29,212	$35,236	$39,517	$43,304	$47,923	$54,130
17	$21,848	$23,666	$26,153	$29,212	$35,236	$40,376	$44,147	$48,803	$55,005
18	$21,848	$23,666	$26,153	$29,212	$35,236	$40,376	$44,147	$48,803	$55,005
19	$21,848	$23,666	$26,153	$29,212	$35,236	$40,797	$44,994	$49,570	$55,876
20	$21,848	$23,666	$26,153	$29,212	$35,236	$40,797	$44,994	$49,570	$55,876
21	$21,848	$23,666	$26,153	$29,212	$35,236	$40,797	$45,401	$50,240	$56,636
22	$21,848	$23,666	$26,153	$29,212	$35,236	$40,797	$45,401	$50,240	$56,636
23	$21,848	$23,666	$26,153	$29,212	$35,236	$40,797	$47,538	$52,497	$58,805
24	$21,848	$23,666	$26,153	$29,212	$35,236	$40,797	$47,538	$52,497	$58,805
25	$21,848	$23,666	$26,153	$29,212	$35,236	$40,797	$49,197	$54,160	$60,532
26	$21,848	$23,666	$26,153	$29,212	$35,236	$40,797	$49,197	$54,160	$60,532
27	$21,848	$23,666	$26,153	$29,212	$35,236	$40,797	$51,681	$56,669	$63,207
28	$21,848	$23,666	$26,153	$29,212	$35,236	$40,797	$51,681	$56,669	$63,207
29	$21,848	$23,666	$26,153	$29,212	$35,236	$40,797	$51,681	$56,669	$63,207
30	$21,848	$23,666	$26,153	$29,212	$35,236	$40,797	$51,681	$56,669	$63,207

SOURCE: *2000 Uniformed Services Almanac.*

NOTES: Values in YOS 9–12 for E8 and YOS 11–12 for E9 were blank in the almanac; reasonable interpolations were made for those values in this table.

References

2000 Uniformed Services Almanac, Falls Church, VA: Uniformed Services Almanac, Inc., 2000.

2001 Uniformed Services Almanac, Falls Church, VA: Uniformed Services Almanac, Inc., 2001.

Ausink, John, Jonathan Cave, and Manuel Carrillo, *Background and Theory Behind the Compensation, Accessions, and Personnel Management (CAPM) Model*, Santa Monica, CA: RAND, MR-1667-AF/OSD, 2003.

Ausink, John, Jonathan Cave, Thomas Manacapilli, and Manuel Carrillo, *Users' Guide for the Compensation, Accessions, and Personnel Management (CAPM) Model*, Santa Monica, CA: RAND, MR-1668-AF/OSD, 2003.